SEO 101

SEO Guide for Beginners

TABLE OF CONTENTS

Introduction 1

Chapter 1: How Search Engines Work 3

Chapter 2: How People Use Search Engines 6

Chapter 3: The Importance of Search Engine Marketing 9

Chapter 4: The Basic of Search Engine Friendly Design and Development 14

Chapter 5: All About Keywords 22

Chapter 6: SEO and User Experience 27

Chapter 7: Growing Popularity and Links 31

Chapter 8: How to Measure and Monitor SEO Success 35

Conclusion 39

INTRODUCTION

I want to thank you and congratulate you for downloading the book, *"insert book title here"*.

This book contains proven steps and strategies on how to properly use SEO to make your website visible online.

Search Engine Optimization (SEO) is a marketing discipline geared towards improving visibility in non-paid search engine results.

It embraces the creative and the technical aspects needed to achieve better rankings, attract traffic, and improve awareness in search engines.

There are different factors that affect the search rankings, from the content you post in the page to the way other websites add link to you. To put it simply, SEO is a set of strategies to make certain that your website is developed in a way that search engines can easily understand.

However, SEO is not all about creating websites that are friendly for the search engines. It is also about making sure that the website is friendly for real people too.

This book is founded on the principle that websites should be friendly to robots and humans alike.

It is designed to give you the basics of all important aspects of SEO - from identifying the right keywords that drive traffic back to your website, to ensuring that your website is user friendly, to building links, and using the power of digital platforms to market the unique value of your website.

If you are a beginner, you might be confused at this point. Don't worry. This book is written for you. The SEO world can be very complicated, and it is fast-changing. That is why you need to learn the basics, and continue educating yourself so you can use this tool effectively to position your website. Learning the basics of SEO can make a big difference.

Thanks again for downloading this book, I hope you enjoy it!

CHAPTER 1
How Search Engines Work

There are two primary functions of search engines:

1. Crawl and build an search index
2. Provide online users with a list of the sites that they have ranked according to relevance

The World Wide Web is often described similar to a series of stops in a metropolis subway system. Every stop can be a specific document (typically a web page, but also JPEG, PDF, XLS, or other files).

The search engine robots follow a system in "crawling" the whole metropolis to identify all the stops. The website links allow the robots, often called the spiders, to find the billions of documents on the web.

When the engines find these files, they read the content and then save particular pieces of information in large databases, to be retrieved later once a user enters a search query using specific keywords.

In order to achieve the Herculean task of keeping billions of data that can easily be retrieved in seconds, search engine companies have built massive data centers around the world.

These data centers keep thousands of special machines that can process massive quantities of data rapidly. When you use the search engine to find a specific piece of information, you usually demand for quick results.

Even a few seconds delay can be very disappointing nowadays for an average online user. Hence, the search engine companies are always improving their machines and their systems to provide results as fast as they can.

Search engines provide answers. When you perform a web search, the search engine crawls its massive database of files then it will only return to files that are deemed useful, and will rank these files according to relevance and popularity.

Search engines determine relevance by looking for the right words. In the early days of the Internet age, search engines cannot go beyond that this simple method, so the results are often limited.

Over time, web engineers have created systems to better match queries and results.

Today, many aspects affect relevance, which you can learn all about in the succeeding pages of this book.

Nowadays, search engines assume that high popularity of a website, page or a file, the more useful it could be for the user.

This method has been very successful in terms of user satisfaction with the results.

Search engine results are not identified and ranked manually.

Through algorithms or set of mathematical equations, the search engines can identify relevant pages, and then rank them according to popularity.

How to Succeed in Using Search Engines

The algorithms used by search engines are complex, so an average marketer cannot penetrate it to influence the results.

The search engine companies provide basic insight on how they rank the results or drive more traffic. However, they have provided the best practices.

Google recommends the following practices to achieve better rankings:

- Develop websites that are mainly for online users and not for search engine bots. Avoid cloaking or the practice of presenting a different content to engines than you display to users.
- Create a website with clear hierarchy and text links. Each page must be reachable through at a minimum of one static text link.
- Develop useful content and write pages that accurately describe the content. Be certain that the <title> elements and the ALT attributes are accurate and descriptive
- Use keywords to create user-friendly and descriptive URLs. Create one version of a URL to find the document through 301 redirects or the rel="canonical" attribute to identify duplicate content

On the other hand, Microsoft engineers recommend the following practices to get better rankings for Bing:

- Ensure that the content is not buried inside rich media (Ajax, Adobe Flash Player, JavaScript) and make sure that the rich media doesn't conceal links from the spiders
- Make sure that the URLs are clean and uses keywords
- Create content that is keyword rich and match keywords that are relevant to users
- Create fresh content regularly
- Avoid placing the text that you want to be indexed within images. For instance, if you prefer your business name and address to be indexed, be certain that it is not placed inside a picture file

CHAPTER 2

How People Use Search Engines

Knowing your target audience is a crucial element in building an online marketing strategy around SEO.

When you understand your market - what they need, and what they are looking for, you can effectively reach and keep them.

That is why, in building your website, be sure to keep your customers in mind.

There are three kinds of search queries:

1. Transactional Queries
2. Informational Queries
3. Navigation Queries

If you want to buy something, such as a travel package online or you want to watch a video, you are making a transactional query.

If you need information, such as the history of nursing in the US, or find the best Chinese restaurant in New York City, you are making an informational query.

If you want to go to a specific place on the web, such as a Facebook page or the website of the US government, you are making a navigation query.

When a potential customer make a query and stumbled upon your website, will they find satisfaction with what they will find?

This is the main question that the search engines are trying to answer every time you make a query.

The main responsibility of search engines is to provide relevant results to the users.

Hence, it is crucial that you ask yourself what your target customers are looking for and be certain that your website can satisfy their queries.

The Importance of Inbound Marketing

Any website who wants to build on an effective web presence should invest time, effort and resources on SEO.

In looking on the big picture of how people are using search engines, there are remarkable data that you can refer to. Here are interesting facts that may help you to understand how people are using search engines today.

- Google led the US core search market in September 2014 with 67.3% of the searches. This is followed by Microsoft Sites with 19.4 % and Yahoo! with 10.0% (comScore, Inc.)
- The cost of online marketing will approach to $77 billion by year 2016. This amount will represent at least 26% of all advertising budgets combined (Forrester)
- 76% respondents used search engines in finding information about a local business, while only 74% of the respondents used printed yellow pages (Burke, 2011)
- Google sends 90.62% of worldwide traffic, followed by Yahoo! with 3.78%, Bing with 3.72%, Ask Jeeves with 0.36%, and Baidu with 0.35%.
- The number 1 spot in Google search results receives 18.2% of all click traffic, while the second spot receives 10.1 %

These interesting research data leads us to essential conclusions about internet search and search engine marketing. Specifically, it is safe to say the following statements:

- Web search is tremendously popular. With annual growth rate of 20%, it can reach every American that is online, and billions of online users around the globe.

- Web search drives significant traffic for online and offline business
- High position in search engine rankings is important for online visibility and driving traffic

CHAPTER 3

The Importance of Search Engine Marketing

Another crucial aspect of SEO is creating a website that is friendly to both search engine spiders and human users.

Even though world of search engines have become complex, spiders cannot see and understand a web page the same way that the human brain can.

With proper SEO, the engines can determine what every page is all about, and how it could be relevant for the search queries performed by online users.

Some skeptics believe that web engineers will never build a search engine that will require websites to adhere to strict rules just to be indexed and ranked.

They think that anyone would want a system, which can index the websites, parse out the codes, and still find a way to provide relevant results, and not a system that are optimized by an average Joe.

But take a look at this scenario. Imagine you have posted on your website a picture of your pet rabbit.

Anyone with good vision may describe the rabbit as "medium-sizes white rabbit, looks like a male, munching on carrots."

Meanwhile, even the most sophisticated search engine today cannot easily make sense of the photo.

That is why SEO rules allow any average Joe to provide clues that the engines can understand to make sense of the content.

As a matter of fact, adding proper structure that is relevant to your web content is crucial to SEO.

By understanding the capacity and constraints of search engines, you can easily build the proper format, and develop the web content in a way that search engines can easily understand.

Without proper SEO, a website will be hidden to search engines.

The Constraints of Search Engine Technology

As discussed in Chapter 1, the leading search engines are operating on set of principles. Search engine spiders crawl the whole database, follow the links, and index the content.

They accomplish this tedious task with remarkable artificial intelligence, but even with its complexity, it cannot provide all solutions.

There are different technical constraints that may lead to problems when it comes to indexing and ranking.

Constraints in Crawling and Indexing

Duplicate pages. Websites that are using a specific Content Management System (CMS) usually create copies of the same page.

This is a primary issue for search engines that are looking for original content:

- Poor URL structure. If the structure of the website link is not digestible for the search engine, there's a possibility that it may not crawl all website content. By chance that the website has been crawled, the content may not be indexed as relevant

- Web forms. Search engines cannot complete online forms, so any content that can be accessed after completing this form will be hidden
- Web blocking. If the website contains errors in the crawling directives, it could lead to blocking the search engines completely, so it cannot be indexed
- Rich-Media Format. Even though search engines are now getting better in reading non-HTML text, the content embedded in rich media is still difficult for spiders to index. This includes text in images, video, audio, Flash files, and plug-ins.

Constraints in Matching Queries

- Language. Search engines read color and colour differently. So if your market is in UK, you need to use the appropriate word in the content
- Inconsistent contextual signals. For example, if the title of your blog post is "New York's Best BBQ Grill" but the article itself is about a hotel resort in Maldives that also carry the same name of the restaurant, the inconsistent messages will send confusing signals to the bots.
- Contradictory locations. Targeting content in French when most people who are visiting your website are from US.
- Rare words. Text that are not written in simple terms that people use to search. For instance, posting content about "portable device used for 24/7 communication" when people are actually searching for cellphones.

Make Certain that Your Content Is Visible

It is critical to get the technical details of a website that is friendly to search engines. However, once you learn the basics, you also need to promote your content. Search engines don't know how to evaluate the quality of the web content.

Rather, search technology depends on the metrics of importance and relevance, and they gauge these metrics by keeping track of what users are doing, what they find and how they react.

You can't just develop a website and upload interesting content. You also need to market that content so it will be shared online.

The Competitive Nature of Search Engines

If you take a closer look at a search engine results page (SERP), you will understand why search engine marketing will last for a long time.

On an average, there are 10 positions on the SERP. The pages that fill these positions have been ranked by the search engine.

The higher position you land on the SERP, the higher your click rate will be, so you can drive more traffic back to your website.

The top three positions receive higher traffic compared to those who are on the lower pages.

The mere fact that there is so much effort devoted in this listing means that there will always be a monetary reward for ranking in SERP.

Regardless of how web search may change in the future, websites will continually compete to get the higher positions.

The SEO World Is Constantly Changing

In the early days of search engine marketing (mid-1990s), using meta keywords, article submissions, and keyword stuffing were all conventional strategies required to get a higher rank.

In 2004, link building using anchor text, getting links from automated blog comments, developing inter-linking farms of websites, and spams, are used to gain high ranking in SERP.

In 2011, vertical search inclusion and social media marketing became the main strategies for SEO.

Search engine companies have continually improved their algorithms along with these changes, so the strategies that are effective in 2004 could damage your ranking today.

There's no way we can predict what will happen in the future. But in the World Wide Web, change is constant.

Hence, search marketing will still enjoy a top spot for those who want to be competitive.

CHAPTER 4

The Basic of Search Engine Friendly Design and Development

Even with the increasing computing power of search engines, they are still constraints when it comes to web crawling and interpreting content.

A web page will look differently to search engine spiders.

In this chapter, you will learn the particular technical aspects of developing web pages so they are designed for both human visitors and search engines.

Be sure to share these details with your web designers and programmers so that you are all on the same page when it comes to developing user-friendly and robot-friendly website.

Develop Web Content that Can Be Indexed by Search Engines

In order to get better visibility for search engine listings, your most essential content must be in HTML text format.

Take note that flash files, java applets, photos, and other non-text content are not given value by search spiders, in spite of recent development in web crawling.

The best way to make certain that the keywords you present to your visitors are also visible to search engines is to display them in HTML.

But there are recent strategies that you can use if you want better visual display and great formatting:

- Add search boxes with crawlable and navigation links
- Add Java plug-ins of Flash with HTML text on the page
- Add alt text for picture. Be sure to assign photos in jpg, gif, or png with alt attributes in HTML so that search engines will have a clue on what the picture is all about
- Add transcript for audio and video content if the words and phrases are indexed by the search engines

Develop Your Website in a Way That Is Visible for Search Engines

Most websites have considerable issues with indexable content, so you need to double check.

You can use valuable tools such as Google's cache tool so you can see what elements of the content that is indexable and visible to the engines.

Using this tool, you may see that for the search engine, a website may not display all the rich information that you see. This affects the search engine's ability to interpret relevancy.

Websites that are all built on flash could be seen by search engines as a blank spade.

So the page is not indexable, and even the links cannot be navigated by crawlers. Without HTML content, it is difficult to rank a page in search engine results.

It's ideal to not only check for HTML content but also use valuable SEO tools to make certain that the pages that you are building are also visible to the search engines. This is applicable to links and images.

Add Links that Are Crawlable

Search engines need to see content to list the pages in their large database indexes.

But before they can do that, they also need to crawl the links first. Making sure that the links are crawlable is crucial to make sure that the pages can be found on a website.

Many websites are using erroneous link structure making the website inaccessible, blocking its opportunity to be indexed.

Excellent keyword targeting, interesting content and effective marketing will become useless if the search engines cannot find your pages.

Anatomy of a Crawlable Link

<a href="http://www.usa.gov.com">Business Gateways</a>

Link tags may contain pictures, texts, or other elements that provides a clickable area on the web site that users can click to visit another page.

There links are the foundation of internet navigation and they are known as hyperlinks. In the above link, the "<a" tag signifies the start of the link. The "http://www.usa.gov.com" is the referral location that tells the search engines where the link is pointing.

Then, the displayed part of the link for the online user or the anchor text provides description about the business gateways available in the United States. Finally, the "</a>" closes the link to contain the text between the tags and also to avoid the link from affecting other elements in the website.

This is the ideal structure of a link, because it can be understood by the search engines.

The web spiders will understand that they must add this link to the link graph of the website and use it to determine the query-independent factors such as Google Page Rank, and follow it to index the relevancy of the webpage.

No Follow Attribute

Rel="nofollow" attribute can be used in the following link syntax

<a href="http://www.usa.gov" rel="nofollow"> John Smith Business Blog</a>

Links may have different attributes, and the search engines almost devalue all of them, with the crucial exception of the nofollow attribute.

In our example above, adding the nofollow attribute to the link will instruct the search engines that the website doesn't want this link to be counted as an endorsement of the reference page.

The nofollow tag was originally used as a strategy to help in blocking automated blog comments and spams.

But as time goes by, it became a special instruction for search engines not to count any value that will regularly be passed.

Links that are added with nofollow are interpreted differently by search engines, but it is certain that they don't carry much value as regular links.

Nofollowed links are now integral in the diverse link profile of search engine database.

A webpage with different inbound links may earn numerous nofollowed links, and it doesn't have any negative effect on the page ranking.

As a matter of fact, high ranking sites have the tendency to accumulate higher percentage of inbound nofollow links compared to websites with low ranking.

On-Page SEO

Keyword usage and targeting are still integral part of the ranking algorithms of search engines, and you can use effective strategies for using keywords to help you in developing well-optimized web pages.

Here are ideal practices when you are doing on-page optimization.

- Add the keyphrase in the title tag at least once. It is best to keep the keyphrase as close as the start of the title tag.
- Add the keyphrase once near the top of the web page.
- Use the keyphrase at least two or three times, including its variations in the body of the page.
- Use the keyphrase at least once in the alt attribute of a photo included in the page. This will help you in both web search and image search that can also drive traffic back to your website.
- Use the keyphrase at least once in the meta description tag. Take note that this is not used by search engines for rankings, but this will help you to attract more links, as the meta description is used by search engines to describe the link.
- Avoid keyword cannibalization or using keywords in link anchor text in reference to other pages of your website.

Title Tags

The title of a website should provide a short and accurate description of the content of a website. It is essential for both search engine optimization and user experience.

As they are crucial in SEO, you can use the following strategies for creating title tags. These strategies cover the essential steps to optimize title tags for usability and SEO.

Add main keywords close to the front. This will help you in getting better page ranking, and it will entice more users to click the results.

Keep It Short. Search engines can only display 65 to 75 characters of the title tag in search results. Beyond that, the engine will only display ellipsis.

This is also the limit allowed by most social media platforms, so following this length is recommended.

But if you are targeting different keywords or long-tail keywords, and including them in the title tag is crucial to get high ranking, it is better to go longer.

Don't forget branding. You can end each title tag with the brand name of your website, because it also helps in improving brand awareness, and develop higher click-through rate for people who are loyal to the brand.

There are instances that it seems good to place the brand at the start of the title tag such as the home page.

Because words at the start of the title tag have more value, take note of what you are targeting for.

Don't forget emotional appeal and readability. Title tags should be readable and descriptive.

Remember, it will be the new visitor's primary interaction with the brand and it must convey only positive image.

Developing a persuasive title tag could help in enticing attention on the SERP, and drive more visitors back to your website.

Never forget that SEO is not all about the technical rules of optimization. It is more of about user experience.

Meta Tags

Meta tags are used to provide more information about the content of a websites. Below you can find the most common meta tags including their use.

Meta Description

Meta descriptions are short text describing the content of the web site.

Basically, search engines don't use the keywords or phrases in this tag for ranking, but these descriptions are the main reference for the text snippet shown under the listing in the results page.

The meta description functions as the advertising copy that may attract the readers to visit the website.

Writing effective meta description is a crucial aspect of search engine marketing. The description should be readable, compelling and uses essential keywords.

If you will notice, Google bolds the keywords you have used in the description.

You can write descriptions at any length, but search engines often cut the text beyond 160 characters, so it is recommended to keep this limit.

Without meta descriptions, search engines will source out snippet from other text elements of the page. For web sites that are targeting several keywords, this is a good strategy to use.

Meta Robots

Meta Robots could be used to give instructions to search engine spiders on a per-page basis. There are different ways to use Meta Robots to control how search engines will interpret a web page.

nofollow/follow instructs the engines if the links on the page will be crawled.

If you choose to use "nofollow", the search engine will devalue the link on the page for searchability and ranking.

Without the nofollow attribute, the search engine will assume that the links should be followed and will do so.

noarchive can be used to put restriction to search engines from caching a copy of the page.

As a default, the spiders will secure visible duplicates of all the indexable pages that are accessible to searchers through the cached link in the results page.

noydir/noodp are specialized tags that instruct the engines not to grab a descriptive snippet of a page from the directory displays of search engines

noindex/index instructs the search engines if the page must be crawled and maintained in the database for retrieval.

If you add the noindex attribute, the page will not be included in the index. As a default, the engine will assume that all pages can be indexed, so using the index attribute is not necessary.

Meta Keywords Are Not Useful Today

In the past, meta keywords are valuable in SEO, but today they have been devalued thanks to the increasing search technology of search engines.

CHAPTER 5

All About Keywords

Keywords are crucial in SEO. They serve as the fundamental element of search and web language.

As a matter of fact, keywords serve as the foundation of the whole technology of data retrieval. As the search spiders crawl the text of the web pages all over the internet, they monitor the web pages in indexes that are based on keywords instead of keeping almost 30 billion pages in one massive data center.

Instead, smaller data centers holding millions of pages are assigned with a specific word or phrase provides the search engines with the capacity to retrieve information in split seconds.

Hence, if you like your website to have the higher chance to rank in results page for "bags", it is best to make certain that the word "bag" is included in the crawlable text of your web page.

Keywords are crucial on how we interact with search engines. In using a word or a phrase on search box, the engine will match the webpages in reference to the words that you have used.

Spelling, capitalization, punctuation and even word order offer added factors that the search engines use to assist you in retrieving the ideal web pages and determine its rank.

Search engines gauge how the keywords are placed on web pages to help in measuring the relevance of a specific file to a search query.

The best way to optimize the ranking of a web page is to make certain that the keywords that you prefer to rank are included in text, titles, and metadata.

In general, as you specify your keywords, you can get a better chance of winning the popularity contest for search results and achieve higher ranking.

For example, you'll have millions of competitors when you use "bags" as your keyword, but there is less competition in the key phrase "Korean handmade bags".

Stop Keyword Stuffing

Since the early days of online search, people have performed abuses in using keywords in a crooked goal of manipulating the search engines.

This includes keyword stuffing. However, this strategy will harm your website today.

In the past, search engines solely depend on keyword use to determine the relevancy of the web page without considering how the keywords are actually used in the page.

Nowadays, even though search engines are still not able to understand the text similar to a human brain, the increase in computing power has allow the algorithms to imitate this function.

The ideal strategy is to use keywords in a natural way.

If your site targets the keyphrase "New York Vacation" then you can include natural content about New York, the best hotels in New York, and the tourist attractions in New York.

Meanwhile, if you just add the keyphrase "New York Vacation" randomly in your page with immaterial content such as a page containing information on rose planting, your entire efforts to be ranked for New York Vacations will be useless.

The essence of keyword use is not to get high ranking for all the keywords within your niche, but to get high ranking for keywords that your target audience is using to search when they need the content from your website.

Keyword Research

Online search all starts when a user types words or phrases into the search box. Keyword research is an integral part of search engine marketing.

Achieving high rank for the right set of keywords could become the deciding factor for your website's success.

With comprehensive research of the demand of your target market, you will learn the words or phrases to target with optimization, and you can also learn more about your market.

Effective SEO is not all about driving more visitors to the website. It is about getting the right type of visitors.

Proper keyword research can even help you project the changes in the market, respond to these changes, and develop the content, product, and services that your market is looking for online.

How to Evaluate a Keyword

It is crucial to determine the value of a keyword to your website. If your page is selling computers do you sell more from visitors searching for "brand new apple macbook" or "refurbished apple macbook"?

The keywords used by your customers to visit your website can be accessed by webmasters, and there are also keyword research tools that will allow you to access this information.

But keep in mind that these tools will not show you the direct value of receiving traffic from these searches.

In order to evaluate a keyword, you need to understand the website, make some theories, do some experiments, validate, and then make conclusions.

Steps to Evaluate a Keyword

1. Ask the following questions:

- Is this word relevant to the content of the website?
- Will visitors find the information that they are searching for on the website if they use this keyword?
- What will be their reaction to the search results?
- Will this keyword provide traffic with monetary or organizational value?

If you have clear answers to the questions above, then proceed to the second step.

2. Find the keywords using leading search engines

Identifying which sites already rank for the keyword that you are targeting will provide you important viewpoint into the current competition, as well as the level of difficulty in ranking for the specified keyword.

Take note of the ads running on the right side and at the top of the results. The presence of these ads signifies that the keyword is valuable, and several ads on top of the organic results could mean a highly profitable keyword.

3. Run a test campaign

If the website doesn't rank for the keyword, run a test campaign to ascertain the conversion. You can use Bing Adcenter or Google AdWords. Select exact match and direct traffic to the matching page of the website. Monitor the conversion rate and impressions of about 250 to 350 clicks.

4. Determine the specific value of every keyword

Using the information that you have already gathered, you can now identify the precise value of every keyword.

For instance, let's say that your ad generated 10,000 impressions daily, of which 200 have visited your website, and six have purchased items giving you total revenue of $600.

Hence, every visitor for the keyword is about $6. The 10,000 impressions for one day may yield a click-through rate of 20-40% with the top rank.

This could mean about 1000 to 2000 daily visits at $6 each or about $ 1 Million to $2 Million per year. Now you know why online businesses are investing more resources to search engine marketing.

Why Use Long Tail Keywords?

Let's use the computer store example again. Is it great to land the top position for the keyword"macbook"?

It's remarkable to use keywords with thousands of searches a day or even hundreds. But in the real setting, these popular keywords usually make up of less than 25% of the online searches.

The remaining 75% of the searches are composed of long tail keywords.

The long tail search is composed of millions of specific searches that could be performed several times in any day, but if you group them together, they now comprise the largest percentage of search volume in the world.

Another interesting fact about using long tail keywords is that they provide better conversion, because they target people who are in the later stage of the purchasing cycle.

A person who is searching for "macbook" is maybe just browsing for more information, and may not even think to buy.

Meanwhile, someone looking for "affordable refurbished apple macbook pro 16GB" probably has their credit card beside the keyboard!

CHAPTER 6

SEO and User Experience

Search engines are investing millions of funds to constantly improve their ability to provide relevant results.

Their intelligence on user experience are continually getting better to simplify navigation, provide information that is closely relevant to the query, visually appealing and accessible to most browsers, and provide valuable content.

In spite of remarkable technological advances, search engine robots still cannot understand text and make sense of pictures and videos the same way we could.

In order to understand and interpret relevance, the spiders depend on meta information about how people will interact with websites, and this provides them some information into the quality of the pages.

The Effect of User Experience and Usability on SEO

There are several factors that search engine spiders could take into account including links, website structure, and keywords.

But through linking patterns, machine learning, and user engagements, the search engines make assumptions on a given site.

User experience and usability are other factors that cause impact on the success of search engine ranking.

They offer an indirect but measurable benefit to the external popularity of the website that the search engine could interpret as an indicator of higher quality.

Developing a friendly user-experience could help in ensuring that visitors to your website will enjoy positive experience and encouraging them to do some actions such as bookmarking, sharing, and inbound links, which are signals that could lead to high search engine rankings.

High Quality and Valuable Content

1. Machine Learning

Google rolled out the Panda update in 2011, which considerably changed the way its algorithms evaluate websites for quality.

The search engine employed human evaluators to manually assess thousands of websites, looking for poor content. It then integrated robot learning to imitate the human evaluators.

When its machines can precisely what humans would assess as a poor quality website, the algorithm was introduced across all websites indexed.

The result was a significant shift that changed the landscape of search engine results.

2. Link Structure

Search engines learned that the structure of the link may serve as a proxy for popularity and votes of confidence.

Premium quality websites and data earned more links compared to their poor quality competitors.

Nowadays, engine algorithms have significantly advances, but these strategies are still effective.

3. Metrics for User Engagement

When search engine retrieves results, it could measure the success of the rankings by keeping track of how you engage with the results.

If the user clicks the first link, then instantly hit the return button to click the second link, this signifies that the user is not satisfied with the first result.

Search engines prefer the long click where the user will not instantly return to the search results page to find another link.

By monitoring millions of queries every day, the search engines have aggregated a high-quality of data to evaluate the quality of the websites.

How to Develop Valuable Content for Effective SEO

You might have already heard the phrase "Content Is King", and this is true. Interesting and valuable content is essential to SEO.

Bear in mind that each search performed at the engines are driven by intent - to learn, buy, find, fix, or to understand.

Search engines put web pages in the results to satisfy this intent.

Developing interesting and comprehensive content, which addresses the needs of the searchers, could improve your chance to achieve top rankings.

Types of Online Searches

There are three main types of online searches: informational, transactional, and navigational.

Informational Searches - Looking for information, getting fast results, or just browsing the web. This type involves a large range of queries from browsing the local news to getting directions to finding out the distance of Mars to the Sun.

Basically, informational searches are mainly not commercialized. Getting the information is the objective of the search, and actions are not required.

Navigational Searches - Visiting a specific website using a pre-determined link.

Navigational searches are performed with the intention of visiting a particular website.

In some instances, the user may not even know the precise link, and the search engine functions as the directory.

Transactional Searches - Determining a local business, buying online, or accomplishing a task.

This type of search doesn't necessarily need a financial transfer.

Signing up to receive a newsletter, creating an email account, or searching for the best vegan restaurant in Chicago are all transactional in nature.

Satisfying these intentions is ideal. Creativity, compelling content, use of appropriate language, and inclusion of photos, audio, or video, could all help in creating content that could fulfill the intention of the user.

You may be rewarded with satisfied searchers who can share their positive experience through website engagement.

CHAPTER 7

Growing Popularity and Links

For search engine spiders that crawl the massive network of the web, links are the streets between websites.

With comprehensive link analysis, the search engines could learn how webpages are related to one another and the nature of these relationships.

Since the early days of the internet age, search engines have considered links as votes of confidence and relevance in the current democratic opinion poll of the web.

Today, link data has become sophisticated, and have used complex algorithms to perform subtle distinction in the assessment of websites and pages in reference on this information.

Although SEO is not all about links, search specialists attribute a massive portion of search engine algorithms to link-related variables.

By using links, search engines will not only assess the popularity of web pages based on the number of links who have voted it, but also spam, credibility, and trust.

Credible websites have the tendency to link to other credible websites, while spam sites receive minimal links from credible sources.

Through this attention on algorithmic use and link analysis, developing the link profile of a website is crucial to gain traction, attention, and drive traffic to the website.

Hence, link building is now a primary task needed to achieve high rank and attract traffic.

Signals Used By Search Engines to Assign Value to Links

In order to know how search engines assign value to links, it is crucial to understand the individual elements of a link, and take a closer look on how the search engines evaluate these elements.

It can be difficult to completely understand the metrics that search engines are using, but if we analyze the patent applications, experimentations, and years of experience, we can make a smart guess that could be applicable in the real-world setting.

Take a look on the list of important factors that you may consider.

These link signals are often noted by professional SEO specialists in measuring the value of a link and the link profile of a website.

FreshRank

Link signals have the tendency to become old over time. Websites that were very popular in the previous decade have faded away in the massive sea of the internet world, and so they don't get fresh links.

Hence, it is crucial to continue accumulating added links. Search engines are now using the freshness of the links to evaluate the present popularity as well as relevance of a website.

TrustRank

The World Wide Web is not entirely clean, as there are numerous spams, about 60% of the web pages.

To effectively filter out irrelevant content, search engines are now using special algorithms to measure trust that is often based on the link graph.

Getting links from highly-credible web pages could result in considerable increase to this metric. Great examples of web pages with high-credible score are government websites, university portals, and non-profit organizations.

Related Links

Spammy links usually go both ways. A website that earned spam links is more often a spammy website itself, and there's a chance that other spammy websites are also linking back to it.

By reviewing these links in the aggregate, search engines could understand the neighboring links in which the website is based on.

Hence, it is recommended to select the sites that you link to and be very careful with websites you try to earn links from.

Local Popularity

Local popularity is based on the principle that links from the websites within a community have more value compared to links with general popularity.

For instance, if you have an online computer store, a link from gadget review site carries more weight than one from a site about fashion.

Worldwide Popularity

The links from popular websites are very valuable.

For example, Wikipedia has millions of diverse websites linking to it, so it has ranked as a popular and relevant websites.

In order to earn credibility and trust, you need the help of other popular websites.

Anchor Text

Anchor text is one of the most important signals that search engines are using in ranking. If hundreds of links point to a page with the targeted keywords, that page could rank well for the keyword.

Social Media Sharing

In the last five years, we have seen a boom in the amount of content shared through social media platforms such as Facebook, Instagram, Twitter, Google+ and Pinterest.

Even though search engines value links that are shared through these platforms differently compared to other kinds of links, they have noticed the growing importance of social media in the present-day SEO.

CHAPTER 8

How to Measure and Monitor
SEO Success

Measuring success in SEO is crucial as it can help you understand if you are on the right track.

Once you measure the result of your SEO efforts, you can improve it.

SEO specialists monitor data about referrals, rankings, and links to evaluate their SEo strategy and establish roadmaps.

Every website is unique, so one factor may carry more weight than the other. However, there is a list of metrics that you can follow to monitor the metrics that are important for SEO.

1. Engine Referrals

The three major search engines (Google, Yahoo!, and Bing) comprise 95% of all search traffic in the US. Outside the US, about 80% of the traffic is generated by Google (except in China and Russia).

Keeping track of the traffic referral from every search engine is crucial because you will be able to effectively compare market share versus your actual performance.

You can also get visibility into significant drops. If the web traffic drops at any given time, understanding the precise and relative contributions from every search engine is critical in diagnosing the issue.

If the traffic coming from Google drops while the other remains at their average levels, there is a high chance that the drop is caused by devaluation of your SEO strategies. If all the engines dropped the traffic, the issue could be accessibility to your website.

Finally, understanding search engine referrals will allow you to discover strategic value.

For instance, one-page SEO strategies such as targeting and keyword inclusion are better used for ranking in Yahoo or Bing compared to Google. Meanwhile, getting particular anchor text links from massive domains is beneficial on Google ranking.

If you can determine the strategies that are successful with one search engine, you will know better on how to refocus your efforts.

2. Referring Visits

It is also essential to monitor the monthly contribution of every traffic source for your website.

This includes referral traffic, direct navigation, and search traffic. Understanding the precise numbers as well as the percentage will help you pinpoint specific weak areas in your campaigns, and will give you a good basis for competitive analysis.

For instance, if you see that traffic has increased considerably but it comes from referral links with poor relevance, it's not time to celebrate yet.

Meanwhile, if the search traffic drops considerably, you might be in trouble. You can use this data to monitor the impact of your marketing campaigns and plan your strategies on how you can acquire more traffic.

3. Keyword Referrals

The specific keywords that drive traffic back to your website are also integral in your SEO analytics.

You need to keep track of these regularly to help you identify emerging trends in the demand of specific keywords, evaluate your performance on key terms, and discover keywords that are getting considerable traffic that you could focus on your efforts in the next campaign.

It is also crucial to find value in monitoring referral counts for keywords outside the top keywords or those that are suitable and relevant to the nature of your website.

If the trend lines are not pointing in the right direction, you will know the strategies you need to implement. Global traffic has increased in the last decade, so a decrease in the volume of referrals could spell trouble.

4. Page Visits

Identifying the number of pages that are receiving web traffic is a crucial indicator for keeping track of the whole SEO campaign.

Based on this number, you can understand indexation or the number of pages from the site that the search engines are maintaining in their database.

For an ecommerce website with more than 50,000 pages, inclusion is critical to acquire traffic, and this metric provides a susceptible number that could indicate the level of success.

As you continually develop the different aspects of your website like link acquisition, meta data, site architecture, site maps, and content originality, you should expect an upward movement signifying that more and more pages are being indexed by the search engine.

More often than not, pages that are receiving search traffic are the best metric you can bank on.

5. Conversion Rate

Conversion is a critical metric because it defines the bottom line of the website's purpose. For instance, let's say that 4.3% of visitors who reach your website using a specific query signed up to receive your newsletter.

With this data, you can check your ranking, and work to improve the position to achieve better conversion.

Because analytics will also tell you what specific page that these visitors have landed on, you can concentrate your efforts in improving the user experience on that page.

The genuine value from this simple metric comes from the initial effort of finding the keywords that are driving visitors who convert to actual customers, and increasing efforts on search rankings, and continually improving the pages that these customers visit.

CONCLUSION

Thank you again for downloading this book!

I hope this book was able to help you to use effective SEO to bring more success to your website.

The next step is to learn advanced strategies on how you can drive more traffic back to your website, develop original and interesting content, and improve user experience.

Finally, if you enjoyed this book, then I'd like to ask you for a favor, would you be kind enough to leave a review for this book on Amazon? It'd be greatly appreciated!

Please leave a review for this book on Amazon!

Thank you and good luck!

www.ingramcontent.com/pod-product-compliance
Lightning Source LLC
Chambersburg PA
CBHW061056050326

40690CB00012B/2645